SCHOLASTIC
ENGLISH SKILLS

Comprehension
Workbook

Ages 8–9

SCHOLASTIC ENGLISH SKILLS

Comprehension

Scholastic Education, an imprint of Scholastic Ltd
Book End, Range Road, Witney, Oxfordshire, OX29 0YD
Registered office: Westfield Road, Southam,
Warwickshire CV47 0RA
www.scholastic.co.uk

© 2016, Scholastic Ltd

456789 89012345

British Library Cataloguing-in-Publication Data
A catalogue record for this book is available from the British Library.

ISBN 978-1407-14180-0

Printed in Malaysia

Acknowledgements

The publishers gratefully acknowledge permission to reproduce the following copyright material: **Andersen Press Ltd** for the use of text and illustrations from *Baker Cat* by Posy Simmonds. Text and illustrations © 2004, Posy Simmonds. (2004, Jonathan Cape); text and an illustration from *The Dragonsitter* by Josh Lacey. Text © 2012, Josh Lacey. Illustration © 2012, Garry Parsons. (2012, Andersen press Ltd); text and an illustration from *Dr Xargle's Book of Earth Hounds* by Jeanne Willis and Tony Ross. Text © 1989, Jeanne Willis. Illustration © 1989, Tony Ross. (1989, Andersen Press Ltd); text and an illustration from *The Steadfast Tin Soldier* by Naomi Lewis. Text © 1986, Naomi Lewis. Illustration © 1991, P.J. Lynch. (1991, Andersen Press Ltd); text and an illustration from *Frog and the Wide World* by Max Velthuijs. Text and illustration © 1998, Max Velthuijs Foundation. (1998, Andersen Press Ltd). **Cambridge University Press** for the use of text and an illustration from *New horizons: Keeping Healthy* by Jacqueline Dineen. © 1994, Cambridge University Press. (1994, Cambridge University Press). **Caroline Sheldon Agency** for the use of text and illustrations from *Leon Loves Bugs* by Dyan Sheldon. Text © 2000, Dyan Sheldon. Illustrations © 2000, Scoular Anderson. (2000, Walker Books Ltd). **Felicity Bryan Associates** and Linda Newbery for the use of text from *Whatnot Takes Charge* by Linda Newbery. Text © 2006, Linda Newbery. (2006, Egmont UK Ltd). **Hachette UK** for the use of text and illustrations from *Seaside Scientist* by Mick Manning and Brita Granström. Text and illustrations © 2004, Mick Manning and Brita Granström. (2004, Franklin Watts). **Macmillan Children's Books** for permission to use text and illustrations from *Room on the Broom* by Julia Donaldson, illustrated by Axel Scheffler. Text © 2001, Julia Donaldson. Illustrations © 2001, Axel Scheffler. (2001, Macmillan Children's Books); text and illustrations from *Ottoline and the Yellow Cat* by Chris Riddell. © 2007, Chris Riddell. (2007, Macmillan Children's Books). **Random House Group Ltd** for the use of text and illustrations from *The Fairytale Hairdresser and Snow White* by Abie Longstaff, illustrated by Lauren Beard. Text © 2014, Abie Longstaff. Illustrations © 2014, Lauren Beard. (2014, Picture Corgi); illustrations from *The Magic Backpack* by Julia Jarman, illustrated by Adriano Gon. Illustrations © 2001, Adriano Gon. (2001, Red Fox); text and illustrations from *Traction Man is Here* by Mini Grey. Text and illustrations © 2005, Mini Grey. (2005, Jonathan Cape); text and illustrations from *UG* by Raymond Briggs. Text and illustrations © 2001, Raymond Briggs. (2001, Jonathan Cape). **Stripes Publishing** for the use of text and illustrations from *Dirty Bertie: Worms!* by Alan MacDonald. Characters created by David Roberts. Text © 2006, Alan MacDonald. Illustration © 2006, David Roberts. (2006, Stripes Publishing). **Troika Books** for the use of the poem 'Rain Dance' from *Blue Balloons and Rabbit Ears.* Text and illustration © 2014, Hilda Offen. (2014, Troika Books). **Usborne Publishing** for the use of text and illustrations from *Beginners: Antarctica* by Lucy Bowman. © 2007, Usborne Publishing Ltd. (2007, Usborne Publishing Ltd). **Walker Books Ltd** for the use of text and illustrations from *Cloud Tea Monkeys* by Mal Peet and Elspeth Graham. Text © 2010, Mal Peet and Elspeth Graham. Illustrations © 2010, Juan Wijngaard. (2010, Walker Books Ltd); text and illustration from *George Flies South* by Simon James. Text and illustrations © 2011, Simon James. (2011, Walker Books Ltd); text and an illustration from *Gorilla* by Anthony Browne. Text and illustrations © 1983, Anthony Browne. (1983, Julia MacRae Books); the cover, a text extract and an illustration from *A Walk in Paris* by Salvatore Rubbino. Text and illustrations © 2014, Salvatore Rubbino. (2014, Walker Books Ltd).

Every effort has been made to trace copyright holders for the works reproduced in this book, and the publishers apologise for any inadvertent omissions.

Images

Page 22, The Boy who cried shark. © Lorelyn Medina/shutterstock.com

Author Donna Thomson
Editorial Rachel Morgan, Anna Hall, Tracy Kewley, Jennie Clifford
Consultants Hilarie Medler, Libby Allman

Cover and Series Design Neil Salt and Nicolle Thomas
Layout Andrea Lewis
Cover Illustration Eddie Rego

Contents

How to use this book

- *Scholastic English Skills Workbooks* help your child to practise and improve their skills in English.

- The content is divided into chapters that relate to different skills. The final 'Review' chapter contains a mix of questions that bring together all of these skills. These questions increase in difficulty as the chapter progresses.

- Keep the working time short and come back to an activity if your child finds it too difficult. Ask your child to note any areas of difficulty. Don't worry if your child does not 'get' a concept first time, as children learn at different rates and content is likely to be covered at different times throughout the school year.

- Find out more information about comprehension skills and check your child's answers at www.scholastic.co.uk/ses/comprehension.

- Give lots of encouragement, complete the 'How did you do' for each activity and the progress chart as your child finishes each chapter.

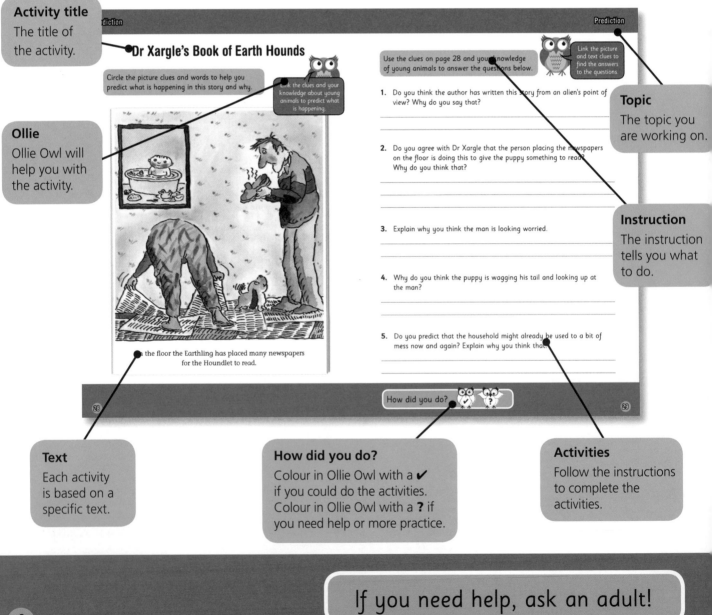

Activity title
The title of the activity.

Ollie
Ollie Owl will help you with the activity.

Topic
The topic you are working on.

Instruction
The instruction tells you what to do.

Text
Each activity is based on a specific text.

How did you do?
Colour in Ollie Owl with a ✔ if you could do the activities. Colour in Ollie Owl with a **?** if you need help or more practice.

Activities
Follow the instructions to complete the activities.

If you need help, ask an adult!

Character, action, place

Read the beginning of the story *Baker Cat* by Posy Simmons.

Who is in the story?
What are they doing?
Where are they?

There was once a cat who belonged to a mean old baker and his lazy wife.
The cat must have had a name, but nobody really knew what it was.
The baker called him:
"Useless!"
"Cloth-ears!"
"Mangy fur-bag!"

The baker's wife couldn't bear cats and kept one only because the bakery was plagued with mice. Mice gave her the screaming shudders.

Use this information to help you to retell the beginning of this story in your own words.

_____

_____

_____

_____

_____

Read the beginning of *Baker Cat* on page 5 again. Answer the questions below. Then ask and answer your own questions about the story.

The answers are right there in the picture and text.

1. What is the main theme of this story?

_____

2. Who knew the name of the baker's cat?

_____

3. What happened to the baker's wife when she saw mice?

_____

4. What did the baker's wife ask the cat to do?

_____

5. Where was the cat when the baker's wife saw the mice?

_____

Your question: _____

_____

Your answer: _____

_____

Your question: _____

_____

Your answer: _____

_____

How did you do?

What's the problem?

Read this page from *The Dragonsitter* by Josh Lacey. Underline the problems that Edward is writing about.

Who and **what** is the story about? What's the problem?

From: Edward Smith-Pickle
To: Morton Pickle
Date: Sunday 31 July
Subject: URGENT!!!!!!!!
Attachments: The dragon

Dear Uncle Morton,

You'd better get on a plane right now and come back here. Your dragon has eaten Jemima.

Emily loved that rabbit!

I know what you're thinking, Uncle Morton. We promised to look after your dragon for a whole week. I know we did. But you never said he would be like this.

Emily's in her bedroom now, crying so loudly the whole street must be able to hear.

Your dragon's sitting on the sofa, licking his claws, looking very pleased with himself.

How do you think Edward might solve the main problem by himself in the end? Draw the problem and write the solution in the boxes below.

Answer the questions below using the clues you have underlined in the text on page 7 to help you. Then retell the story in your own words.

1. Who is having a problem in the story?

_____

2. The main character has more than one problem. Write three of the main character's problems.

    1. _____

    2. _____

    3. _____

3. What does Edward think will solve the overall problem?
Why might this help?

_____

_____

4. What do you think might happen in the end?

_____

_____

5. Retell the story so far in your own words.

_____

_____

_____

_____

_____

How did you do?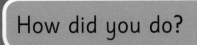

How to make a cake

Read the instructions below that tell you how to make a chocolate cake.
Write the correct number for each baking step in the boxes.
Then answer the questions below.

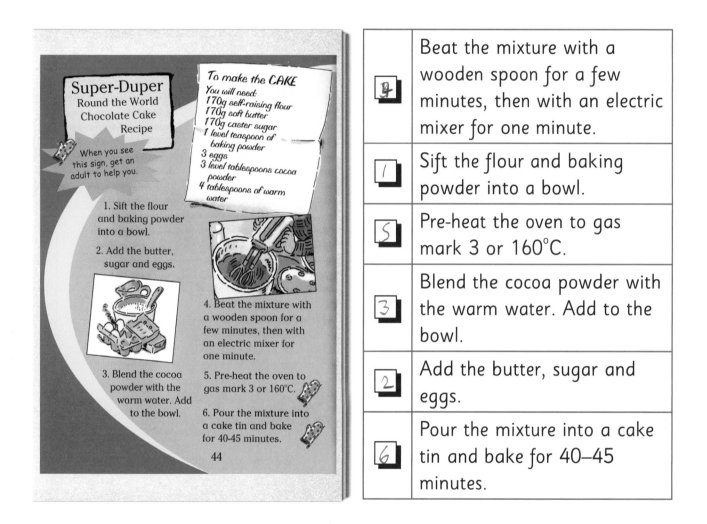

4	Beat the mixture with a wooden spoon for a few minutes, then with an electric mixer for one minute.
1	Sift the flour and baking powder into a bowl.
5	Pre-heat the oven to gas mark 3 or 160°C.
3	Blend the cocoa powder with the warm water. Add to the bowl.
2	Add the butter, sugar and eggs.
6	Pour the mixture into a cake tin and bake for 40–45 minutes.

1. Which ingredients should be in the bowl when you beat the mixture?

The flour, baking powder, butter, sugar and eggs should be in the bowl when you beat the mixture.

2. Should you remove the cake from the oven before or after 40 minutes? Why do you say that?

You should remove the cake from the oven after 40 minutes like it said in the instructions otherwise it might be underbaked.

Read the instructions for making the topping. In your own words, retell the instructions in the correct order in the box below.

To make the TOPPING

You will need:
240g icing sugar
100g dark chocolate
30g butter
3 tablespoons hot water
chocolate flakes

1. Put the dark chocolate and butter in a bowl.

2. Melt them by standing the bowl in a pan of hot water.

3. Gradually beat in the icing sugar and water till it is shiny.

4. Spread the topping over the cake and decorate with chocolate flakes.

First: _Put the dark chocolate and butter in a bowl._

Then: _Melt them by standing the bowl in a pan of hot water._

Next: _____

Finally: _____

Now answer the following question about these instructions. Then ask and answer your own question about making the topping.

Question: What do you need to do first when you make the topping?
Answer: _____

Your question: _____
Your answer: _____

How did you do?

Baker Cat

Read this page from the story *Baker Cat* by Posy Simmons.

Write down what happens in the beginning, middle and end of the story shown in the pictures on page 11.

Who is this story about? **What** is the problem? How is the problem **resolved**?

Beginning: The story is about... (Who? What? Where?)

retelling

Middle: The problem is...

dog

End: I think what happens in the end is...

in secret

Retell the story out loud. Use the phrase in the speech bubble to help you get started.

At the start of the story...

How did you do?

Whatnot Takes Charge

Read about the characters in *Whatnot Takes Charge* by Linda Newbery. Use this information to answer the 'who' question below. Then write your own 'who' question and answer.

'**Who**' questions ask about the characters in a story.

Ajay was working on something for the Art competition, in secret.

Tim was busy with Whatnot. On Monday evening, he and Grandad took Whatnot to his first Obedience Class. Whatnot loved it. All those dogs! All those smiley mouths and waggy tails! He was so excited that he couldn't help dashing in mad circles when he was supposed to be Walking at Heel.

Example:

Question: Who is working in secret?

Answer: Ajay is working in secret.

Question: Who is busy with Whatnot?
Answer: _YOUV_

Your 'who' question: _WHITEOGToⁿKL_
Your answer: _OIZE4V_

The literal '**who**' answers are right there in the text.

Read the following page of *Whatnot Takes Charge* and answer the question. Then write your own 'who' questions and answers about the characters in the story.

Question: Who said 'He'll learn'?

Answer: _____

_____

Your 'who' question: _____

_____

Your answer: _____

_____

Your 'who' question: _____

_____

Your answer: _____

_____

'He'll learn,' said Grandad.

'He's a bad influence!' said a man with a perfectly-behaved beagle called Brodie.

'Give him time,' said Mrs McLeish, the trainer.

How much time? Tim thought. The competition was on Saturday week.

'Sit!' he tried. 'Stay!' Whatnot could never Sit and Stay without wriggling and whimpering, but he was doing his best – until a gust of wind made the door slam.

Your 'who' question: _____

Your answer: _____

Your 'who' question: _____

Your answer: _____

How did you do?

Whatnot Takes Charge

Look for clues in the picture and text below that tell you **what** the characters are doing. Circle any clues in the picture and underline clues in the text. Two have been done for you.

'What' questions ask about the characters' **actions** in a story.

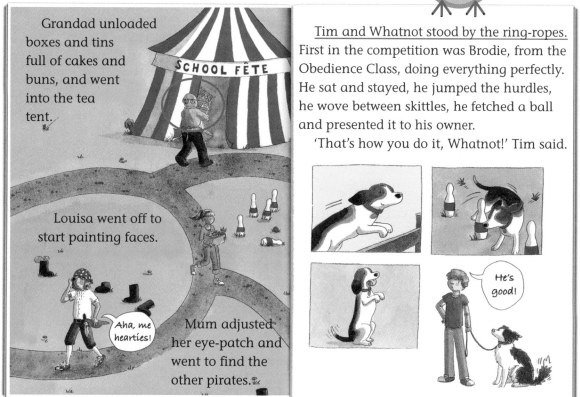

Use the clues you found to answer the question below. Then write your own question and answer about what the characters did at the fete.

Question: What did Grandad do with the cakes and buns?

Answer: _____

Question: What _____

Answer: _____

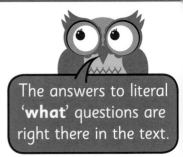

Use the clues that you found in the text and pictures on page 15 to help you answer the questions below. Then ask and answer your own 'what' questions.

The answers to literal '**what**' questions are right there in the text.

1. What did Mum do as she went to find the other pirates?

_____

2. What were Tim and Whatnot doing by the ring-ropes?

_____

3. What did Louisa go off to do?

_____

4. What did Brodie do at the hurdles?

_____

Your 'what' question: _____

Your answer: _____

_____

Your 'what' question: _____

Your answer: _____

_____

Your 'what' question: _____

Your answer: _____

_____

How did you do?

The Fairytale Hairdresser and Snow White

Read this page from *The Fairytale Hairdresser and Snow White*. Then use the words in the box to help you answer the questions below.

'Where' questions ask about the location of the characters, objects and events in a story.

Kittie lacey was the best hairdresser in all the land.

We will make you the fairest of them all!

Miss Peep's Wool Shop

Mermaid's Aquatic Pets

DR T FAIRY CROWNING GLORY DENTISTRY

ALICE'S TEA ROOM

Kittie's Cuts

Customers came from far, far away to have their hair styled, their tails plaited and their beards trimmed.

(on) inside under below opposite by in front of
next to near beside (behind) beneath on top above

Example:

Question: Where is the castle?

Answer: The castle is <u>on</u> the hill <u>behind</u> Alice's Tea Room.

Question: Where is the dragon?

Answer: _____

Use the information on page 17 to help you answer the 'where' questions below. Then ask and answer three of your own 'where' questions using as many words as you can from the list.

Question: Where are Kittie's customers?

Answer: _____

_____

Question: Where is the wool shop?

Answer: _____

_____

Your 'where' question: _____

Your answer: _____

_____

Your 'where' question: _____

Your answer: _____

_____

Your 'where' question: _____

Your answer: _____

_____

How did you do?

Where do you live?

Draw a map of where you live and places nearby. Then ask and answer your own 'where' questions about the places on your map using the words in the box below.

Ask '**where**' questions about information that can be seen clearly on your map.

below	inside	by	next to	between	beneath
opposite	under	in front of	near	behind	on top of

Your 'where' question: _____

Your answer: _____
_____

Your 'where' question: _____

Your answer: _____
_____

Your 'where' question: _____

Your answer: _____
_____

How did you do?

Cloud Tea Monkeys

Red pen for **who**. Blue pen for **what**.
Green pen for **where**.

Read this text from *Cloud Tea Monkeys*. Underline **who** the sentences are about, **what** they are doing and **where** they are in different coloured pens. Then enter this information in the table below. The first one has been done for you.

Tashi dragged the empty basket down to the shade of the tree that grew out of the rocks, and when she got there she sat and wept with her head in her hands. She wept for her mother and for Aunt Sonam and for herself. She cried for a long time. Then she wiped her wet eyes with the backs of her hands and looked up. The monkeys were sitting in the circle of shade, watching her. They were all watching her – the babies hanging from their mothers, the older ones quiet for once, Rajah himself sitting looking at her with his old head tilted curiously to one side. So she told them everything because there was no one else to tell.

Who	What (doing)	Where
Tashi	dragged the empty basket	down to the shade of the tree that grew out of the rocks.
Monkeys	Sitting in a circle of shade	In the circle of shade
baby monkeys	hanging	wh from their mothers
Rajah	Sitting while looking at Tashi	Next to Tashi who was crying

Answers to all the literal questions below are right there in the text.

Use the clues you underlined on page 20 to help you answer the questions below. Then ask and answer your own 'who', 'what' and 'where' questions.

1. Who dragged the empty basket down to the shade of the tree?

Tashi dragged the empty basket to the shade of the tree

2. Where was the tree growing?

The tree grew out of the rocks

3. What did Tashi do in the shade of the tree?

Tashi cried in the shade of the tree

(2)

4. Who was Tashi crying for?

She was crying for her mother and Aunt Sonam horse

5. What were all the monkeys doing?

The monkeys were sitting in a circle of shade

Your 'who' question: _____

Your answer: _____

Your 'what' question: _____

Your answer: _____

Your 'where' question: _____

Your answer: _____

How did you do?

The boy who cried shark

Read the poem. Circle clues in the picture and text that suggest what might happen next because of the boy's actions.

Think how actions create consequences

The boy who cried shark

I am a boy
Who loves the sea,
but I don't like swimming
in company.

They are the folk
Who go each day
Down to the beach
To surf in the bay.

To stop the surfers
Spoiling my fun
Each day I shout 'Shark!'
And watch them run.

While everyone's fussing
I hide the fin.
Then I swim in peace
And ignore their din.

When they look again
The shark is not there,
Just a lad swimming,
How does he dare?

They are so silly
To believe my cry,
When day after day
It's just a lie.

Then one day,
It's not a lie.
'Killer shark, over there!'
They hear me cry.

'Not true!' they say,
'Heard that before.
We don't believe you.
Not any more.'

Explain what is happening in the story so far.

So far, _____

_____

_____

Draw pictures or write notes to show what you think happens next.

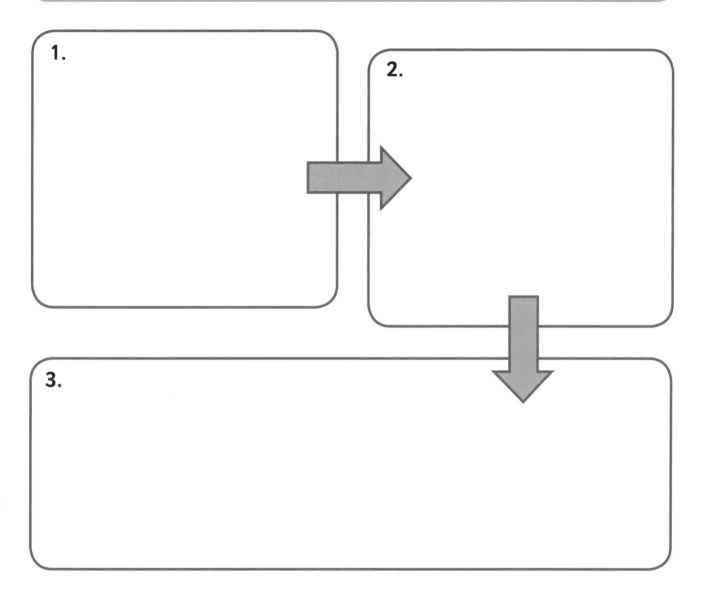

1.

2.

3.

Why do you think this happens? What does the boy learn from this?

I think this happens because _____

_____

_____

_____

_____

How did you do?

Ug – Boy Genius of the Stone Age

Use your knowledge of the Stone Age and clues on the page to make your predictions.

Read this page and circle clues in the pictures and text that suggest what might have happened **before** and what might happen **next**.

Use the clues in the pictures and your knowledge of the Stone Age to help you answer the questions.

1. Why do you think the story is about a boy who lived in prehistoric times?

_____

_____

2. Do you think Dad is cutting up the animal skin to make trousers for his son? Why do you think that?

_____

_____

3. Do you think Ug and his dad have done this before? Why do you think that?

_____

_____

4. What do you think happened before this scene? Why do you think that?

_____

_____

5. Whose idea do you think it might have been to make the trousers out of animal skin?

_____

_____

6. What do you think might happen next? Why do you think that?

_____

_____

How did you do?

Book covers

Look for clues in the title and picture on the cover.

Look carefully at the book cover below.

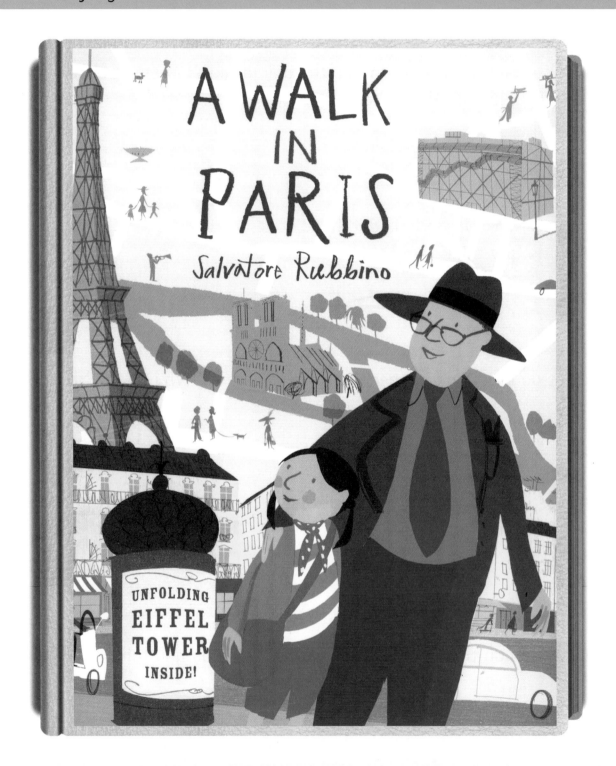

Use the clues on the book cover on page 26 to help you answer the questions below. Then ask and answer your own prediction question.

Look for clues in the cover title and picture to help you answer the questions.

1. What sort of book do you think this is? Why do you say that?

_____

_____

2. From the clues in the title, explain why you think there are two characters on the cover. What might their roles be in the book?

_____

_____

3. From the information on the cover, do you think it is easy to see Paris on foot? Why do you think that?

_____

_____

4. Name one of the places the characters will most likely visit in the book. Why do you think that?

_____

_____

Your prediction question: _____

_____

Your answer: _____

_____

How did you do?

27

Dr Xargle's Book of Earth Hounds

Circle the picture clues and words to help you predict what is happening in this story and why.

Link the clues and your knowledge about young animals to predict what is happening.

On the floor the Earthling has placed many newspapers for the Houndlet to read.

Link the picture and text clues to find the answers to the questions.

Use the clues on page 28 and your knowledge of young animals to answer the questions below.

1. Do you think the author has written this story from an alien's point of view? Why do you say that?

_____

_____

2. Do you agree with Dr Xargle that the person placing the newspapers on the floor is doing this to give the puppy something to read? Why do you think that?

_____

_____

_____

3. Explain why you think the man is looking worried.

_____

_____

4. Why do you think the puppy is wagging his tail and looking up at the man?

_____

_____

5. Do you predict that the household might already be used to a bit of mess now and again? Explain why you think that.

_____

_____

How did you do?

A Walk in Paris

Read this page. Underline 'who', 'what' and 'where' clues in different coloured pens. Think about the literal questions that you could ask using this information.

Red pen for **who**.
Blue pen for **what**.
Green pen for **where**.

I've just seen a street-cleaner turn a big key. Now there's water gushing out of the kerb! "Mind your feet, Grandad!" I say.

"We have these special taps all over Paris," the other man explains. "They give us water for cleaning, right on the street."

Wallace fountains like this one are a familiar sight in Paris, positioned on busy pavements and in squares. Throughout the summer, they provide clean drinking water to anyone who needs it.

Parisian street-cleaners wear green uniforms and drive green vans. Even their brooms are green!

Now circle the **inference** clues on the page that help you think more deeply about what is happening.

Use the picture and text on page 30 to answer the questions below. Tick the PC Page box if it is a literal question. Tick the Text Detective box if it is an inference question.

PC Page looks for **literal** answers that are right there in the picture and text. The Text Detective looks for **inference** answers that link to clues in the pictures and text.

Question	PC Page	Text Detective
1. Who is talking to the girl's grandad? Where are they?	☐	☐
2. Why is the girl warning her Grandad to watch out?	☐	☐
3. Why is the street-cleaner turning the big key?	☐	☐
4. Where would you expect to see Wallace fountains?	☐	☐
5. Do Wallace fountains provide people in the streets with drinking water at the hottest time of the year? How do you know?	☐	☐

How did you do?

Traction Man is Here

Think about how you know what is happening.

Read this page from *Traction Man is Here*. Look for clues that suggest what is happening in the story. Circle the clues in the pictures and underline the clues in the text. One has been done for you.

Use the clues that you found in the pictures and text on page 32 to help you answer the questions below.

1. Are Traction Man and Scrubbing Brush travelling in a space rocket? How do you know?

_____

I know that because _____

_____

2. What time of year is it? How do you know?

_____

because _____

3. Do Traction Man and Scrubbing Brush stay awake throughout the journey? Explain how you know that.

_____

_____

4. Are Traction Man and Scrubbing Brush the only ones in 'suspended animation' in the back seat? How do you know?

_____

_____

5. How else does the boy entertain himself on the journey? What are the clues that suggest this?

_____

_____

How did you do?

Seabirds

Read the text and circle the clues that explain why rubbish is dangerous to seabirds. Use the circled clues to help you complete the sentence below in three different ways. One has been done for you.

Then answer the detective question below.

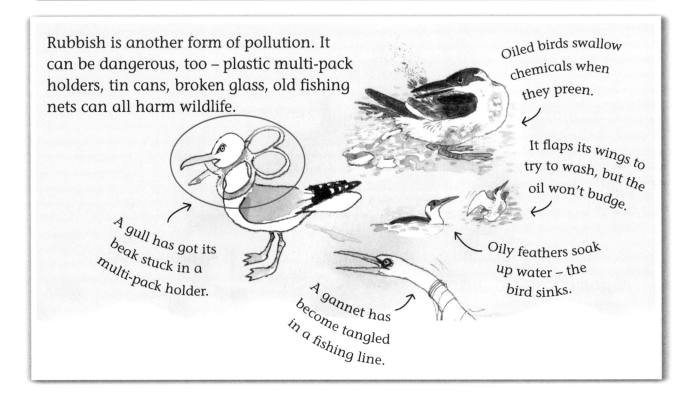

Rubbish is another form of pollution. It can be dangerous, too – plastic multi-pack holders, tin cans, broken glass, old fishing nets can all harm wildlife.

Oiled birds swallow chemicals when they preen.

It flaps its wings to try to wash, but the oil won't budge.

A gull has got its beak stuck in a multi-pack holder.

Oily feathers soak up water – the bird sinks.

A gannet has become tangled in a fishing line.

Rubbish is a danger to seabirds **because**...

1. ...their heads can get stuck in plastic multi-pack holders.

2. _____

3. _____

Detective question: Is litter a threat to seabirds? Explain how you know.

Answer: _____

_____

_____

Circle the clues in the text that explain the special features of each seabird.

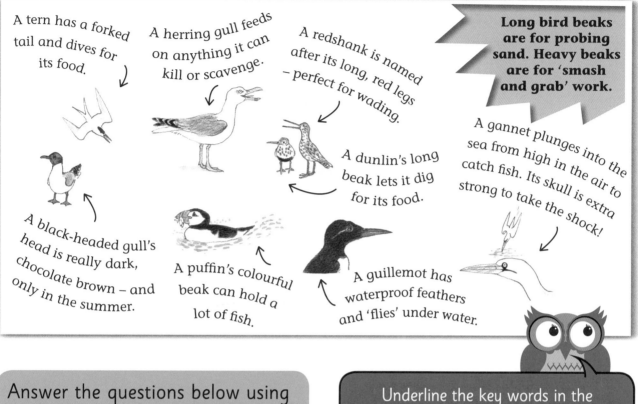

A tern has a forked tail and dives for its food.

A herring gull feeds on anything it can kill or scavenge.

A redshank is named after its long, red legs – perfect for wading.

Long bird beaks are for probing sand. Heavy beaks are for 'smash and grab' work.

A dunlin's long beak lets it dig for its food.

A gannet plunges into the sea from high in the air to catch fish. Its skull is extra strong to take the shock!

A black-headed gull's head is really dark, chocolate brown – and only in the summer.

A puffin's colourful beak can hold a lot of fish.

A guillemot has waterproof feathers and 'flies' under water.

Answer the questions below using 'because'. Use the clues you have circled to explain how you know.

Underline the key words in the questions before you search for answers in the text and picture clues.

1. Do gannets have a <u>tough skull</u> to help them dive into the sea? How do you know that?

_____

_____

_____

2. Do dunlins search for food deep in the sand? How do you know that?

_____

_____

_____

How did you do?

Leon Loves Bugs

Read the text. Circle or underline the clues on the page that suggest **what** the characters are doing, **where** they are and **why**. Then write the clues in the box below. Two have been done for you.

"Mrs Leary!" shouted Natasha. "Mrs Leary! Leon's playing with bugs again!"
Mrs Leary looked over the heads of the other children.

"Leon Mittel!" called Mrs Leary. "Whatever you're doing, stop it this minute!"

Leon stuck his tongue out at Natasha, then turned to Mrs Leary. "Me?" he asked innocently. "I'm not doing anything."

The rest of the class stepped aside as Mrs Leary marched towards Leon. Mrs Leary knew better than to believe that Leon wasn't doing *anything*. Leon Mittel was always doing something.

"What's that behind your back?" she demanded.

Leon dropped the dazed caterpillar on the grass.

"Nothing." He held up his hands.

playing with bugs

looked over the heads of the other children

Answer the questions below using the clues that you found in the text on page 36. Use 'because' to explain how you know. Then write your own detective questions and answers.

Underline the key words in the questions before you search for answers in the text clues.

1. Who is fascinated by bugs? How do you know that?

_____

_____

2. Is Leon right at the back of the other children? What clue suggests this?

_____

_____

Your detective question: _____

_____

Your answer: _____

_____

Your detective question: _____

_____

Your answer: _____

_____

Your detective question: _____

_____

Your answer: _____

_____

How did you do?

Compound words

A compound word is when two words are put together to make one word.

Read the text and look at the picture from the book *Journey* by Aaron Becker. Underline the **compound words** in the text and then match them to the meanings below. One has been done for you.

Every <u>weeknight</u> in the summer my friend Jim races over the railway bridge to meet me at the crossroads near my house. Sometimes we cycle to the seaside together on his tandem bike to swim in the sea, collect seashells and have an ice-cream in the last of the afternoon sunshine. Other times we ride to the countryside nearby and sit amongst the buttercups and daisies watching dragonflies dancing over the cool stream till sunset. Our imaginary bluebird watches over us as we cycle homeward at the end of each day exhausted but happy.

Example:
weeknight = evening during the week

_____ = close

_____ = fields/woodland

_____ = beach

_____ = yellow flowers

_____ = junction

_____ = occasionally

_____ = insects

Think about the meaning of the compound words in the story and answer the questions below. Then ask and answer your own clarification question about one of the compound words in the text.

1. Match the words in boxes **a.** and **b.** to make new compound words. Write the new words in box **c**.

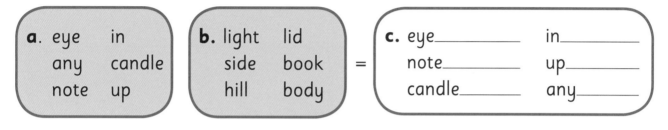

a. eye   in
     any   candle
     note   up

b. light   lid
     side   book
     hill   body

=

c. eye_____ in_____
    note_____ up_____
    candle_____ any_____

2. Choose two compound words from the text or from the list above. For each one, write a simple sentence that explains its meaning.

   1. _____

   2. _____

3. In the story the boy and girl 'cycle homeward at the end of the day'. What does the author mean by the word 'homeward'?

_____

4. Do the boy and girl go down to the seashore every so often? Explain how you know that.

_____

_____

Your clarification question: _____

_____

Your answer: _____

_____

How did you do?

The Steadfast Tin Soldier

Look at the picture and read the text. Circle the words in the text that have a similar meaning to the words in the boxes below. Then write the word from the text in the correct box.

Synonyms are words with similar meanings. **Antonyms** are words with opposite meanings.

Example:

tiny	miniature
small	undersized

The word is <u>little</u>.

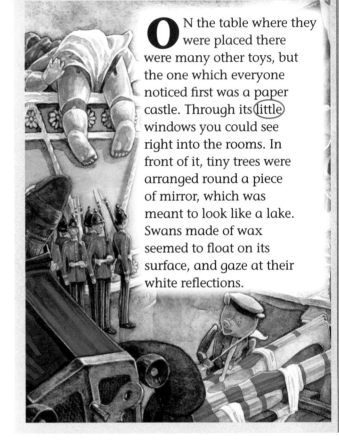

ON the table where they were placed there were many other toys, but the one which everyone noticed first was a paper castle. Through its (little) windows you could see right into the rooms. In front of it, tiny trees were arranged round a piece of mirror, which was meant to look like a lake. Swans made of wax seemed to float on its surface, and gaze at their white reflections.

countless	umpteen
numerous	lots of

The word is _____.

organised	placed
gathered	positioned

The word is _____.

Draw lines to match the words from the text with opposite meanings.

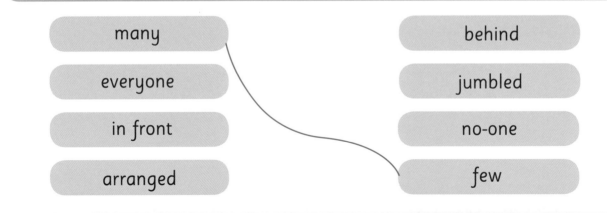

many	behind
everyone	jumbled
in front	no-one
arranged	few

Remember to look for synonyms and antonyms in the questions and text to help you answer.

Look again at the text on page 40 and then answer the questions below.

Example:

Question: Did <u>more than one</u> person <u>spot</u> the paper castle? How do you know that?

Answer: Yes, <u>everybody</u> <u>spotted</u> the paper castle because it says that '<u>everyone</u> <u>noticed</u> the paper castle'.

1. Were there just a few other toys on the table? How do you know that?

_____

_____

2. Were the tiny trees placed behind the castle? Explain how you know.

_____

_____

3. Was the lake scene a bit of a jumble? Why do you say that?

_____

_____

4. The text says: 'Swans made of wax seemed to float on its surface, and gaze at their white reflections.' Rewrite the sentence replacing the word 'gaze' with another word that has a similar meaning.

_____

_____

How did you do?

Seaside safety

Look at the pictures and read the text about seaside safety in Australia.

Skimming = identifying main ideas.
Scanning = searching for key words.

seaside safety

Sharks are magnificent – and some types can be dangerous when they think swimmers are tasty seal pups! But sharks are rare – there are a lot of other seaside dangers you should be much more careful about.

Dos and Don'ts

- Don't climb on cliffs or explore caves without an adult to supervise you.
- Don't swim unless you're with an adult and don't try to dodge big waves as they break on the beach. They could sweep you away. See the shark bite for more advice about safe swimming.
- Look out for stinging jellyfish and other poisonous beasties, such as weaver fish.
- Wash your hands after a day on the beach – microscopic germs love to live in the sand and sea water at the seaside.

Skim and scan to find the words below in the text. Circle or underline the words as you find them in the passage. One has been done for you.

sweep	dodge	think	microscopic
supervise	tasty	dangerous	magnificent
careful	swimming	rare	poisonous

Remember the answer is right there in the text and pictures.

Use the words you have underlined or circled in the text on page 42 to help you answer the questions below. Then ask and answer two of your own literal questions.

1. What is this passage about?

_____

_____

2. When are some types of shark dangerous?

_____

_____

3. What shouldn't you do without adult supervision?

_____

_____

Your literal question: _____

_____

Your answer: _____

_____

Your literal question: _____

_____

Your answer: _____

_____

How did you do?

Room on the Broom

Skim and scan the text below to find **synonyms** (words with similar meanings) for the words in the box. Draw a line to match the similar words. One has been done for you.

Read the text aloud using the synonyms instead of the original words. Does the text still make sense with these words?

Similar words (synonyms)

lengthy

lofty

beamed

soared

howled

fiercely

displayed

perched

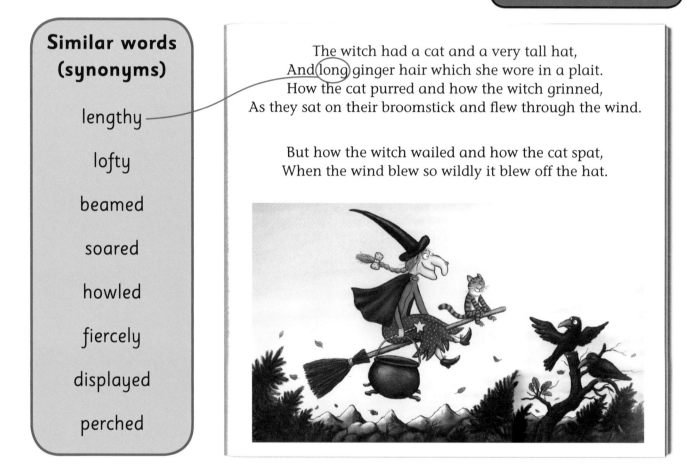

The witch had a cat and a very tall hat,
And (long) ginger hair which she wore in a plait.
How the cat purred and how the witch grinned,
As they sat on their broomstick and flew through the wind.

But how the witch wailed and how the cat spat,
When the wind blew so wildly it blew off the hat.

Write antonyms (words with opposite meanings) for these words.

Example: wildly: *gently*

long: _____

blew: _____

wailed: _____

sat: _____

purred: _____

Skim and scan the text on page 44 to help you answer the questions below. Underline the key words in the questions that link to similar or opposite meanings in the text.
The first one has been done for you.
Then ask and answer your own inference question using synonyms and antonyms.

Skimming means identifying main ideas. Scanning means searching for key words.

Example:
Question: Was the witch's hair <u>short</u> and <u>messy</u>? How do you know?

Answer: No, the witch's hair was not short and messy because it says she had '<u>long</u>' hair 'which she wore in a <u>plait</u>'.

1. Who was beaming as the witch and her cat soared through the wind on their broomstick?

_____

_____

2. Was the wind blowing so fiercely that the witch lost her hat? How do you know that?

_____

_____

Your inference question: _____

_____

Your answer: _____

_____

_____

How did you do?

Gorilla

Read this extract from *Gorilla* by Anthony Browne. Think about how the words explain the characters' feelings.

Look closely at the picture. Think about what the body language tells you about how the characters are feeling.

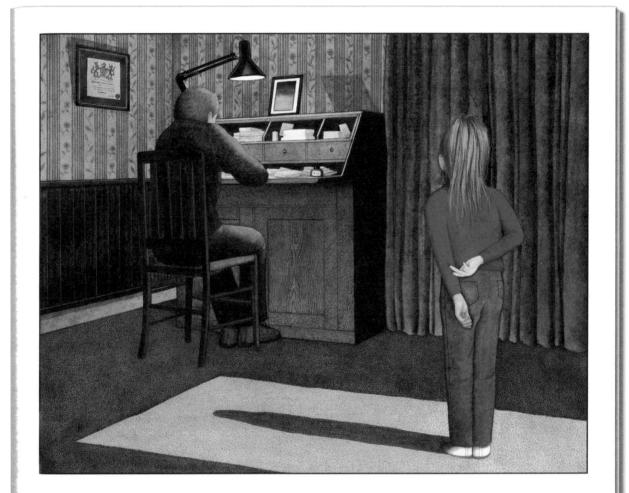

He went to work every day before Hannah went to school, and in the evening he worked at home.

When Hannah asked him a question, he would say, "Not now. I'm busy. Maybe tomorrow."

Answer the questions below. Underline the clues in the questions to help you find the answers in the picture and text on page 46.

Then ask and answer your own evaluation question about what the characters are doing, how they are feeling and why.

Evaluation questions have no right or wrong answer – as long as you link your ideas to the information in the story.

1. Do you think Hannah is worried about disturbing her dad while he is working? Why do you say that?

_____

_____

2. How do you think Dad is feeling in this scene? Why do you think that?

_____

_____

3. Do you think Dad sees very little of Hannah? How do you know that?

_____

_____

4. How do you think Hannah feels when Dad says "Not now, I'm busy. Maybe tomorrow". Explain why you think that.

_____

_____

_____

Your evaluation question: _____

_____

Your answer: _____

_____

How did you do?

Cloud Tea Monkeys

Read this extract from the book *Cloud Tea Monkeys*.

Look for the 'who', 'what' and 'where' information in the text and the pictures. Circle clues that explain what is happening and how the characters are feeling. Two have been done for you.

(The next morning was the same.) Tashi knew that if her mother could not work there would be no money. With no money to pay the doctor, her mother would not get well. If her mother did not get well, she could not work and there would be no money. The problem went round and round. It was like a snake with its tail in its mouth and Tashi was frightened by it.

When her mother was asleep again, Tashi dragged the heavy tea-basket to the door. She found that if she leant her body forward she could lift the bottom of the basket off the ground. Bent like this she began the long walk to the plantation.

Use the clues from page 48 to help you answer the questions below. Then ask and answer your own literal, inference and evaluation questions.

Literal question: Who is this story about?

Answer: _____

Inference question: Is Tashi's mother ill? How do you know that?

Answer: _____

_____

Evaluation question: What does Tashi do to try to solve the problem? How do you know that?

Answer: _____

_____

Your literal question: _____

Your answer: _____

Your inference question: _____

_____

Your answer: _____

_____

Your evaluation question: _____

_____

Your answer: _____

_____

How did you do?

49

Frog and the Wide World

Look at the picture and read the text. What do you think Frog and Rat are thinking? Write their thoughts in the speech bubbles below.

When morning came, Frog didn't want to get up. But Rat was firm, and off they set, up hill and down dale, into the wide world. "Are we nearly there *now*?" panted Frog.

"Not nearly," said Rat. "If you want to see anything of the wide world you have to persevere."

Evaluation questions have no right or wrong answer – as long as you link your ideas to the information in the story.

What do you think the characters are feeling and thinking? Answer the questions below. Then ask and answer your own evaluation question.

1. Why do you think Frog was reluctant to get up in the morning?

_____

_____

2. Do you think Frog or Rat is the leader? Why do you think that?

_____

_____

_____

3. Do you think Frog has travelled far from home before?
   Why do you think that?

_____

_____

4. Do you think both characters are feeling impatient at this stage of the journey? Explain why you think that.

_____

_____

Your evaluation question: _____

_____

Your answer: _____

_____

Dirty Bertie

Look at the picture and read the extract from *Dirty Bertie*. Circle or underline the clues in the text that might explain how the characters are feeling and why. The first clue has been underlined for you.

Bertie looked at Nick. Nick looked at Bertie. <u>Both of them eyed the last slice</u> of fudge cake. Then Nick did a surprising thing – he offered the plate to Bertie.

"You have it, Bertie," he said with a sickly smile. "I don't mind, really."

Bertie wasn't going to fall for that one. "That's okay, Nick, I want you to have it."

"Oh, well if you insist," said Nick. "We don't want it going to waste." He snatched the last piece and took a large bite. "Thanks, Bertie."

Bertie glared furiously. He'd been tricked! Well, that was it. No more manners, this was war. That fudge cake was his by right and he was going to get it back. Bertie reached into his pocket and brought out his hanky. Nick was too busy talking to Miss Prim to notice a hand dart across the table.

"Any second now," thought Bertie. "Five, four, three, two..."

Nick reached for the cake and raised it to his mouth. There was something black on top.

"ARGHHHHH! A fly!" screamed Nick, dropping the cake on the table.

"ARGGHHHH!" shrieked Miss Prim as Buzz landed in front of her.

"I'll get it!" cried Miss Skinner. She seized a spoon and attacked the blue bottle.

Use the circled text clues from page 52 and your own experience to help you answer the questions below. Remember to underline key words in the questions. Then ask and answer your own evaluation question.

Evaluation questions have no right or wrong answer – as long as you link your ideas to the information in the story.

1. Why do you think Bertie and Nick made a point of looking at each other as they 'eyed the last slice of fudge cake'?

_____

_____

2. Do you think Nick really wanted Bertie to have the cake when he offered it to him? Why do you say that?

_____

_____

3. When Bertie thought he 'wasn't going to fall for that one' what did he mean? Why do you say that?

_____

_____

4. Why do you think Bertie felt 'the fudge cake was his by right'?

_____

_____

Your evaluation question: _____

_____

Your answer: _____

_____

How did you do?

George Flies South

Look at the picture and read the text.

Whilst George waited, a strong gust of wind

swept through the park.

It tore through the branches

scattering the leaves everywhere.

George's nest wobbled …

Use the text and picture on page 54 to help you answer the questions below. Think about the different question types.

1. Who is this story about and where does it take place?

_____

2. What is George doing?

_____

3. Why do you think George is sitting alone in his nest?

_____

_____

4. What time of year do you think it is? How do you know?

_____

_____

5. A strong gust of wind 'tore through the branches'. Tick the word below that has a similar meaning to the word 'tore'. It must make sense in the story.

☐ flowed   ☐ ripped   ☐ slipped   ☐ ran

6. Do you think George is feeling safe in his nest in the tree? Why do you think that?

_____

_____

7. What do you think might happen next? Why do you think that?

_____

_____

How did you do?

Seasons

Look at the pictures and read the information on the page.

plums   raspberries   cherries   strawberry

Summer heat

In the drowsy heat of summer,
ants march, **dragonflies** dance,
and **mosquitoes** buzz.
Juicy **fruits** are ripe for picking and for making
into yummy summer foods and drinks.

ants

stay warm

Some animals prefer hot, dry weather. Lizards lie back and soak up the heat of the Sun to keep warm.

14

Use the text and picture on page 56 to help you answer the questions below. Think about the different question types.

1. What is this information about?

_____

2. Name the fruits that are ripe for picking in the summer.

_____

3. Give examples of the types of summer foods and drinks that you could make from one or more of these fruits.

_____

_____

4. Do lizards enjoy sunbathing in the summer? How do you know that?

_____

_____

5. The author talks about 'the drowsy heat of summer'. What do you think they mean by the word 'drowsy'? Tick the correct box below.

☐ sleepy   ☐ chilly   ☐ awake

Write your choice of word for drowsy in this phrase:

'In the _____ heat of summer...'

6. Do you think insects enjoy the sunshine in the same way as lizards do? Why do you think that?

_____

_____

_____

How did you do?

Frog and the Wide World

Look at the picture and read the text.

Rat chose a comfy spot and they both lay down to rest.
"Rat," said Frog after a little while, "I can't sleep."
"Close your eyes and think of your favourite things,"
said Rat.
Frog tried but it didn't work. He could hear strange
noises. It was probably lions . . . or tigers.

Use the text and picture on page 58 to help you answer the questions below. Think about the different question types.

1. Explain what is happening in this part of the story.

_____

_____

2. What did Frog and Rat do after 'Rat chose a comfy spot'?

_____

3. 'Rat chose a comfy spot'. Which of these words has the opposite meaning to the word 'comfy' in the text?

☐ quiet ☐ prickly ☐ snug

Write your choice of antonym in this sentence:

'Rat chose a _____ spot.'

4. Who is more used to sleeping outside? How do you know?

_____

_____

5. Do you think Frog has a lively imagination? Why do you think that?

_____

_____

6. What do you predict happens next in the story? Why do you think that?

_____

_____

How did you do?

Antarctica

Look at the pictures and read the information about Antarctica.

A land of ice

Antarctica is the coldest and windiest place in the world. Most of the world's ice is in Antarctica.

It is so cold that every winter the sea around Antarctica turns to ice.

In summer some of the ice melts and rocky beaches appear by the sea.

There are dry valleys where no snow falls. They are the driest places on Earth.

Only the tallest mountains can poke through Antarctica's thick ice.

Read the information on page 60 again. Then answer the questions below. Think about the different question types and underline the clues in the questions.

1. What is this information about?

_____

2. Where is most of the world's ice?

☐ In the dry valleys   ☐ In Antarctica

3. Are there places on Antarctica that are free of snow and ice sometimes? How do you know that?

_____

_____

_____

4. Why do you think only the tallest mountains can poke through Antarctica's ice?

_____

_____

5. Which of these words has a similar meaning to the word 'cold' in the text?

☐ mild   ☐ freezing   ☐ stormy

6. Do you think Antarctica would be a good place to visit? Why do you think that?

_____

_____

How did you do?

Rain dance

Look at the picture and read the poem.

Rain-Dance

The seagulls are doing their dance again –
Wings clasped to their sides, they stare up the street.
Up and down, up and down, go their knobbly pink knees;
And boom-diddy-boom! drum their heavy webbed feet.

"Hey!" whisper the worms in the dry, blackened earth.
"Can you hear the rain fall – pitter-pat! Pitter-pat?
Let's get some of that – let's hurry! Let's go!"
And they wriggle on up to the rat-a-tat-tat!

While over their heads, the dancers pound on;
Their golden beaks shine in the midsummer heat –
Intent on their dance, in a world of their own;
And boom-diddy-boom! go their heavy flat feet.

"Come on!" call the worms. "It's raining up there!
There'll be rich, fruity earth – we'll have it for tea."
Out pop their heads in the shimmering air.
Dart! Snap! and swallow! How wrong can you be?

Use the poem and picture on page 62 to help you answer the questions below. Think about the different question types.

1. What is this poem about?

2. What are the seagulls doing when they drum their heavy webbed feet on the ground?

3. What do the worms think is happening above them when the seagulls are dancing? How do you know that?

4. Why do you think the worms are excited that it might be raining?

5. Are the seagulls quick to grab the worms as they surface? How do you know?

Use the poem and picture on page 62 to help you answer the questions below. Think about the different question types.

6. The seagulls are 'intent on their dance'. Tick the correct box that has a similar and opposite meaning to 'intent' here.

synonym (similar): ☐ focused ☐ bored ☐ happy

antonym (opposite): ☐ settled ☐ undecided ☐ busy

7. The poem says the seagulls were 'intent on their dance, in a world of their own'. What do you think this means?

_____

_____

8. What do you think this poem tells us about seagulls?
Why do you think that?

_____

_____

_____

Now write your own question and answer about the poem and picture on page 62. Tick the box next to the type of question you have written.

☐ literal question   ☐ inference question   ☐ evaluation question

Your question: _____

_____

Your answer: _____

_____

How did you do?

Food poisoning

Look at the picture and read the information.

Food poisoning

Food poisoning is quite separate from other illnesses. It strikes very suddenly. It is caused by eating food which has been **contaminated** by bacteria or viruses.

Someone with food poisoning has bad stomach pains and is very sick. This is the body's way of getting rid of the contaminated food. (Stomach pains and sickness can be the symptoms of other illnesses as well.) A doctor would normally suspect food poisoning if a person has been well until eating a meal, or if a group of people who have eaten the same food are all taken ill.

How is food contaminated?

Food can be contaminated in different ways. Most cases of food poisoning are caused by bad hygiene. Food should always be thoroughly cooked to kill bacteria.

Dirty kitchens and food that is going bad are breeding grounds for bacteria.

Frozen food should be thawed out completely, otherwise bacteria may not be killed when the food is cooked.

34

What can you see here that could cause food poisoning?

Use the text and picture on page 65 to help you answer the questions below. Think about the different question types.

1. Why is a dirty kitchen a problem for health?

_____

_____

2. What are the symptoms of food poisoning?

_____

_____

3. What are the possible causes of food poisoning in this kitchen scene.

_____

_____

_____

_____

_____

_____

4. Can it be difficult sometimes for doctors to know if you have food poisoning? How do you know that?

_____

_____

5. Is it important not to undercook some foods? Why do you think that?

_____

_____

_____

Use the text and picture on page 65 to help you answer the questions below. Think about the different question types.

6. Food can be 'contaminated' in different ways. What does the word 'contaminated' mean? Tick the correct meaning below

☐ contained   ☐ polluted   ☐ clean

7. 'Frozen food should be thawed out completely.' Tick the words that have similar and opposite meanings to 'thawed out'.

synonym: ☐ stiff   ☐ loose   ☐ defrosted

antonym: ☐ melted   ☐ frozen   ☐ soggy

8. What do you think you should always do before preparing or eating food to avoid food poisoning? Why do you say that?

_____

_____

Now write your own question and answer about the text. Tick the box next to the type of question you have written.

☐ literal question   ☐ inference question   ☐ evaluation question

Your question: _____

_____

Your answer: _____

_____

How did you do?

Ottoline and the Yellow Cat

Look at the pictures and read this extract from *Ottoline and the Yellow Cat* by Chris Riddell.

She lived in Apartment 243 with Mr. Munroe, who was small and hairy and didn't like the rain or having his hair brushed.

Ottoline, on the other hand, loved all kinds of weather, particularly rain, because she liked splashing in puddles. She also liked brushing Mr. Munroe's hair.

LIKES SPLASHING IN PUDDLES AND COLLECTING THINGS

SMALL, HAIRY AND FROM A BOG IN NORWAY

She found it very relaxing, and it helped her to think, especially if there was a tricky problem to solve or a clever plan to work out.

Ottoline liked solving tricky problems and working out clever plans even more than she liked splashing in puddles. She kept her eyes and ears open in case she came across anything unusual or interesting. So did Mr. Munroe.

A MOUSE CALLED ROBERT THAT MR. MUNROE CAME ACROSS IN THE KITCHEN LAST TUESDAY

OTTOLINE'S NOTEBOOK, WHERE SHE JOTS DOWN THINGS SHE SEES AND WORKS OUT CLEVER PLANS

Use the text and pictures on page 68 to help you answer the questions below. Think about the different question types.

1. Who shares an apartment with the main character in the story?

_____

2. Where did Mr. Munroe live before he moved into Apartment 243?

_____

3. Does Mr. Munroe enjoy wet weather? How do you know that?

_____

_____

4. Do you think Ottoline has good detective skills? Why do you think that?

_____

_____

5. 'She kept her eyes and ears open.' Explain what the author means by this phrase.

_____

Now write your own question and answer about the text. Tick the box next to the type of question you have written.

☐ literal question   ☐ inference question   ☐ evaluation question

Your question: _____
Your answer: _____
_____

How did you do?

Sea shells

Look at the pictures and read the information.

Sea shells

Everyone collects empty shells when they go to the seaside. Shells are the 'outside skeleton' of animals called shellfish. The shells protect these animals' soft bodies. After shellfish die, their shells are often washed up on the beach – for us to find!

Razors dig themselves deep into the sand.

Barnacles grow on rocks, boats and even other animals' shells.

Mussels grow in tightly packed colonies.

Whelks are scavengers. Some prey on other shellfish.

Crabs have shell over their backs, legs and pincers.

Scallops can 'swim' by squirting water through their shell.

Winkles, like most shellfish, feed on seaweed.

Otter shells live in the same spot all their lives.

Limpets cling tightly to their rocky homes.

Cockles live in sandy beaches – as many as 10,000 in 1 square metre.

Use the text and pictures on page 70 to help you answer the questions below. Think about the different question types.

1. What are sea shells?

_____

2. Which is the least adventurous of the shellfish? How do you know?

_____

_____

3. What might you expect to see attached to your boat if you left it on the seashore for any length of time? Why do you think that?

_____

_____

4. 'Whelks are scavengers. Some prey on other shellfish.' What does the word 'scavengers' mean here? Tick the correct meaning below.

☐ nasty   ☐ cowards   ☐ hunters

Now write your own question about the text. Tick the box next to the type of question you have written.

☐ literal question   ☐ inference question   ☐ evaluation question

Your question: _____

Your answer: _____

_____

How did you do?

Progress chart

Colour in Ollie when you have completed the chapter.

1 Retelling	**2** Literal questioning	**3** Prediction
7 Review	**6** Evaluation	**5** Clarification	**4** Inference

CONGRATULATIONS!

Name: ....

You have completed the

Comprehension

Workbook

AGES 8–9

Age: ....   Date: ....